D0517710

michael james art & inspirations

C&T PUBLISHING

Copyright © 1998 Michael James

Developmental Editor: Barbara Konzak Kuhn

Technical Editor: Joyce Engels Lytle

Cover Design: John Cram

Book Design: Lesley Gasparetti

Contributors: Patricia Harris and David Lyon, Patricia Malarcher

Photography by David Caras unlesss otherwise noted.

Photo credits:

James Beards, pp. 63, 67, 70, 71, 72, 79

Paul E. Deegan, APSA; MNEC, p. 83

Eric Gentil, pp. 132, 133

Joanne Rapp Gallery/The Hand and the Spirit, Scottsdale, p. 80

Sharon Risedorph, p. 87

JoAnn Sieburg-Baker, pp. 52, 64

Chee-Heng Yeong, p. 69

All rights reserved. No part of this work covered by the copyright hereon may be reproduced or used in any form or by any means—graphic, electronic, or mechanical, including photocopying, recording, taping, or information storage and retrieval systems—without written permission of the publisher.

Part of the contents of this book was previously published in different form by Editions Victor Attinger, SA, of Neuchâtel, Switzerland, under the title *Michael James: Studio Quilts*.

Plexiglas is a registered trademark of Rohm & Haas Company.

Library of Congress Cataloging-in-Publication Data

Michael James: art & inspirations.

    p.   cm.

    Includes index.

    ISBN 1-57120-040-1

    1. James, Michael,—Criticism and interpretation.

I. James, Michael

NK9198.J26M53   1998

746.46'092—dc21   97-44777

                              CIP

Published by C&T Publishing, Inc.

P.O. Box 1456

Lafayette, California 94549

Printed in Hong Kong

10   9   8   7   6   5   4   3   2   1

contents

When I look over this body of work that I'm still in the process of producing,

one thing strikes a recurring note: this work is part of a life, my life, and my life is what it is

because it is shared with a sensitive and caring and loving individual

who reminds me, just by her being, how lucky I am. So, this is for Judy, my shining light.

preface

The work documented in this book represents nearly twenty-five years of personal and artistic development that had its roots, I think, in the purchase of Marrguerite Ickis' *The Standard Book of Quilt Making and Collecting* when I was an undergraduate art student in the late 1960s. I was in the habit of browsing my favorite bookstore each weekend, not always with particular titles in mind, and one Saturday I came across an inexpensive paperback edition of that classic work and found myself seduced by the strong graphic patterns shown on its pages. I certainly had no plan to make a quilt at the time, and I wouldn't have known how if I'd wanted to, but I decided to add the book to my small library so that I could revisit those lively images at my leisure.

Well, large oaks do in fact grow from small acorns. One thing led to another, and by the time I was in graduate school my interest in quilts had solidified to the point where I began making patchwork in my spare time as a way of relaxing from the stress of the workload my studies and starting a family had brought to my life. The fact that my wife Judy was an avid sewer and needleworker helped: there was fabric around the house, along with all the tools I might need, and there was her encouragement and support.

I liked the quiet, meditative quality of the work, and I also liked the idea that this non-toxic medium posed far fewer health risks to myself or to my young family than the paints and solvents and other materials associated with my painting and printmaking activities.

Within three months of getting my graduate degree in painting, I had stopped that work entirely in favor of quiltmaking. The decision to commit myself to fabric didn't happen overnight, but slowly grew on me over a period of many months. After having spent six years in art school, I found that I had very ambivalent feelings about the nature of the so-called "fine" arts that I'd been focused on for so long. I'd been influenced by a widely held notion at the time that painting and sculpture were somehow disciplines that occupied a rarified atmosphere superior to lowly "handcrafts." As student painters I and my colleagues had come to believe that ours was a "calling," that we were involved in the work of the mind and the spirit, work that shadowed the humble work of hands. When we described something as "too crafty" we were sending signals to each other that process was secondary and that any association with craftwork was to be discouraged.

I gradually came to see these misguided notions for what they were, not least because of the exposure I had to a range of craft disciplines in the studios of the School for American Craftsman at Rochester Institute of Technology where I did my graduate work in painting. There some of the most respected faculty in their fields taught committed student craftspeople the ins and outs of wheel-thrown pottery, hand-loomed fiber, and metalwork and jewelry, several of the strongest craft areas at that school in those days. During my second year at RIT, in fact, I worked in the ceramics area, as a graduate assistant making clay bodies for students in the evening program. It was far from a prestigious job, but it put me in close contact with the makers in that department and helped me to understand the dignity inherent in the work of hands.

So, my headlong move into the quilt arena was inspired, at least in part, by a reactionary impulse. But it was also conditioned by the rich history surrounding quiltmaking, a history that I was discovering through intensive research that took up a good part of my spare time. I scoured libraries and bookshops, magazines and newspapers, searching for anything I could find on quilts and quilt history. There would clearly be no turning back.

It's hard now, nearly twenty-five years later, to remember the open-mouthed awe with which I approached the first quilt shows we attended, and the inspiration that I carried away from them. I've seen so much in the meantime, and have moved from being a hobbyist to a full-time careerist, and the innocence and wonder that characterized that period of discovery is now only a faint memory. I know it still must be that way for many people who, today, are discovering quilts for the first time. I envy them that wide-eyed sense of discovery, that first blush of enthusiasm and excitement when they discover, as I once did, that this is the medium they'd been searching for.

That I have been able to build a solid and successful artistic career in this field is something about which I am very grateful. Many artists struggle throughout their lives with little recognition and few rewards for their work. Few artists have the luxury of being able to do their work and stay focused on that work, and often have to give themselves to other careers to buy time for their studio work. I've been lucky that my "job" revolves around quilts: designing and making them, and teaching others in workshops about ways to approach the creation of late-twentieth-century quilts. I'm happy to have been able to make a contribution to the metamorphosis in thinking about quilts and quilt art in the last two decades, and I'm honored and gratified to have contributed to the body of work that will bridge two centuries of ongoing quilt activity.

Students often ask me how they might build careers in this field. "What should I do if I want to become a full-time quilt artist?" I think that if I'd had to ponder that question when I first launched my involvement I would have been at a loss to come up with an answer. I never set about to have a career. I just took one step at a time, letting one thing lead to another. There was no program, no set goal. There was no plan. There still isn't. It was then, and still is, just a matter of doing the work.

If I can offer any practical advice today to someone who wants to pursue quilts as a studio art activity, I would say simply: "Do the work." Just do it. The commitment ultimately has to be to the work. Everything else is secondary. It's so easy to make excuses for not working, for not producing, that some people manage to give themselves over to making excuses and they never get any real work accomplished. So, making has to be the priority, and the energies of the artist's mind and heart and hands have to be concentrated on the materials and the processes that occupy and enliven the studio or workshop.

Artists' thinking about their work changes and metamorphoses over time, just as the work itself does. No artist wants to run in place, stuck on one idea or bound to one style or image. This is why opening oneself up on a continuing basis to as many influences and exposures and experiences as possible is so important to the serious artist. For quiltmakers in particular, it's critical to look beyond the specific medium with which we're involved. There is a natural tendency in any discipline to stay focused on the navel. What's absolutely necessary is to go for the broader picture: to learn about other disciplines, to follow what's going on in theater and literature and music and politics and religion, to talk with and interact with people who have different preoccupations or who come from different backgrounds and traditions. The artist who is able to do this brings much more diversity in thought and concept to his or her work, and the unique re-working and filtering of those varied exposures through the individual artist's sensibilities is what provides the underpinning for original and inventive studio work.

Michael James
Somerset Village, Massachusetts

michael

"I started out BELIEVING that there

was enough inherent DIGNITY and

VALUE in the medium, in its HISTORY

and its METHODS, to justify a dedi-

cated and continued INVOLVEMENT."

james @ work

Fabrics for a new strip panel are selected from my stock and arranged in varied groupings based on color, value, or intensity contrasts and usually represent graded runs that form a natural sequence.

◄ Cut strips are secured together in groups of 36 to await piecing into panels, as time permits.

Once a grouping of 36 fabrics is chosen and arranged to complete a strip panel, it is divided into groups of nine fabrics and these are cut all at once using a rotary cutter and a Plexiglas® straight edge.

9

A full-size cartoon is drafted on large sheets of paper, following the approximate design sketched in the small maquette at right. The outlines of all major forms as well as the diagonal stripes are indicated.

After the strips are sewn together, they are pressed, first from the back side (leaving seams open) and then from the front.

I cut the individual paper forms from the cartoon using a sharp cutter. These forms each serve as pattern pieces for cutting the fabric shapes from the strip-pieced panels.

"Since my work deals with COLOR and

LIGHT, it could be realized in paint.

But that isn't all that the work is

about—only part of it. It's also about

an ALTERNATIVE to the mainstream,

The collection of some 70 panels, plus fragments and odd pieces, are laid out for easy access during the construction of the quilt top. These panels are made up of strips that finish at 1" wide, and are used for larger quilts. I also work with an equivalent collection of panels that finish at $^3/_4$" wide, for use in constructing smaller quilts.

about choices made so that the PER-

SONAL and the PROFESSIONAL, the

growing of relationships as well as the

growing of a career, could CO-EXIST."

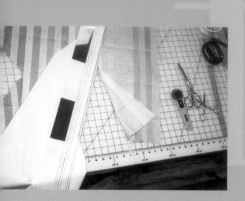

The paper pattern pieces are pinned to the panels and the fabric shapes are cut. The Plexiglas ruler is marked with indications for cutting strips of different sizes and also for adding seam allowance where needed, as on this shape.

"I MAKE quilts because I have a long-standing and sincere interest in the form itself and because I LOVE fabric —I love to FEEL it and to HANDLE it and I ENJOY the sewing processes with which fabrics are secured TOGETHER."

Along curved edges,
seam allowance is
added by measuring
with a ruler and mark-
ing the cutting edge.

Cutting the
fabric shape.

The fabric shapes
are pinned to the
studio wall in the
spaces left after
removal of the
pattern piece from
the cartoon.

Pinning of the fabric shapes to the wall allows for on-going evaluations of the work-in-progress and for frequent changes and alterations that become necessary as new shapes are added and the piece changes and develops.

"When I made my first quilt twenty years ago the popular IDEA of what a quilt SHOULD BE was defined by centuries of what we think of as 'tradition.' I've tried over the years to broaden that popular definition, to suggest what a quilt CAN BE."

Once all of the fabric shapes are in place and design problems resolved, the piecing of the top begins, using pins to align seams for precise joints.

As shapes are
pieced together,
the seams are
pressed consis-
tently open.

Piecing a
pinned seam.

heaven

HELL

"HEAVEN is now, in one's STUDIO.

So is HELL."

◄ View in the studio.

The backing fabric
is stretched tightly
across the table
surface and secured
with push pins
along its outer sides.

Once the quilt top
is completed, the
backing fabric is
laid out in prepara-
tion for securing
the three layers of
the quilt.

The batting is laid
over the backing,
followed by the quilt
top. The top is
smoothed out, and
then the seams
defining the main
forms are adjusted
for correct curvature
or straightness and
pinned through to
the backing.

A tailor's basting is used to secure the principal seams so that they will not shift or distort during the quilting process. Basting always takes longer to accomplish than the quilting itself, but the care and attention here is important for accuracy in the final product.

The basted quilt is rolled and the quilting is begun using nylon monofilament as the surface thread and cotton-covered polyester thread in the bobbin. A walking foot is used to prevent creeping of the top layer relative to the backing.

"I feel that CONTROVERSY of any kind can ultimately be beneficial, since it often gives rise to QUESTIONING, to DIALOGUE, to PROBLEM-SOLVING, and to GROWTH. I have tried over the years to stimulate all of those things in regard to quilts and quiltmaking, and as I look back over the last quarter century, I think we really have come a LONG WAY in the quilt world."

I prefer to quilt from the outside edges, moving in to the middle of the piece, because I've learned that this method helps to reduce any distortion in the overall shape of the quilt.

the

ideas of order

of

the

art

"The most important thing is to LOVE,

and to be loved. The second most

important thing is to DO THE WORK."

# of michael james

It's been a quarter century since Michael James started stitching quilt blocks as a way to relax while working on his Master of Fine Arts thesis at the Rochester Institute of Technology. During that period, he has transformed himself from a painter looking for relaxation through a soothing fiber tradition to one of the artists most closely associated with the "art quilt" or, as Michael prefers to call it, the "studio quilt" movement.

Not long after he received that M.F.A. in 1973, Michael effectively retired his brushes in favor of needle and thread as the medium to continue his explorations of color and of the interplay of visual movement and illusions of space. Already well-versed in the traditions of fine arts that form a part of an academic training in painting, he immersed himself in the quilting tradition. It was a fortunate time because popular books depicting historical quilts were just becoming available, and serious academic research into American quilts was getting into high gear.

Michael approached quilting much as he had approached painting—as a body of work to assimilate and make his own. In effect, he learned from the folk art of quiltmaking much as other 20th century artists had learned design, color and compositional lessons from African and Asian folk art. And like those other artists, Michael brought the modern artist's preoccupations and intellectual framework to his own work.

There's a lot of misunderstanding about exactly what kind of artist Michael James is— maybe because he gives equal weight to his fine arts training and to the grand tradition of quilting. He is both a modern artist and a quilter. In his mind, that dual status poses no conflicts. To Michael, the medium is irrelevant—art lies in what you do with it. But he also insists on applying the demanding yardstick of professional artistry.

Creativity is a wonderful thing, but it doesn't become art until it has been tempered by an understanding of other great art and hardened through the discipline of aesthetic standards.

Michael insists on equally high standards of workmanship. Just as a painter must be able to draw, an artist working in the quilt medium must be able to piece and sew. Sloppy points and ragged stitches betray the vision of the work. Mastery of technique is admirable, but for an artist, it's a given. The real question is what the artist does with those skills: yet another Dresden Plate or Drunkard's Path—or an original composition that functions as a work of art in its own right, respectful of the medium but not limited by tradition?

Quilting requires craft, and Michael apprenticed himself to it as any craftsperson must. He made traditional blocks in time-honored patterns. He cut and sewed and hand-quilted. He learned about surface texture through the impressive quilting of his monochromatic *Night Sky 1*. In other words, he paid his dues by repeating the lessons, the techniques and the patterns of traditional quilting. But he also brought that art-school training to bear on every lesson. As a result, his questions about quilting moved quickly beyond *How did they do that?* to *What can I make it into?* Soon after he took up quilting in earnest, Michael began a series of formal and aesthetic explorations that continue to this day.

Michael's art-school training in the late 1960s and early 1970s came at a critical moment in American art—a period when abstraction had become the new orthodoxy and representational art was considered hopelessly naïve. (Obviously, the academic point of view has shifted again in the intervening years.) Fine Art (with a capital "F" and a capital "A") wasn't "about" anything except itself. The formal and technical aspects of the art were, in fact, also the content.

That's not to suggest that Michael even shares those views—but the hard-edged intellectualism and formalism of his training point a direction for his work. And they proved to be a fertile preparation for his radically different approach to the quilt as a medium for fine art.

Night Sky I, 1977,
74" x 90"

Some of the design considerations of traditional quilts neatly intersect the concerns of modern art, especially in the handling of geometric forms and the interplay of color. It could be argued that anonymous quilters working in a domestic folk art intuitively tackled certain technical problems of geometric assemblage and interrelationships of color long before most modern artists articulated them as formal "problems" at all.

Issues of geometry and color arise, in large part, from the nature of the "materials." In the pieced quilt tradition, colored pieces of fabric are usually subdivided by folding and cutting, then reassembled in patterns that emphasize contrast of color and sometimes of form. The cloth is almost always woven cloth—which is to say that it is a medium defined by its perpendiculars of warp and weft. Thus, most traditional pieced quilts in the U.S. have elaborated on the design possibilities of linked squares, rectangles and the triangles that result from dividing squares and rectangles diagonally. Less common, but hardly

unknown, are more visually complex designs that begin with a circle and section it, again folding and cutting.

In all these approaches to quilting geometry, creation of the forms is independent of absolute measure—all units of measurement are relative. Instead of using a yardstick, many traditional quilters began by folding the end of a length of cloth diagonally to produce a square and then further subdividing it from there. In effect, size of pieces and their relationship to each other were established by the cloth, not imposed by some external measurement. You could say that traditional quilters cut their suits to fit the cloth.

As Michael has pointed out in his lectures, quilting is an art form of construction—of building up patterns from smaller pieces in the way a contractor builds a house. Its dimensions can expand or contract as the quilter wants them to; they are not fixed in the way that a painter's canvas on a stretcher is fixed. At the same time, the pieces of a traditional quilt are fixed in repetitive forms. Because a quilter keeps building with these forms (which could be blocks or strips), the quilter inevitably becomes immersed in the possibilities and limitations of geometry. It also means that a quilter, using her or his own experience, tends to design patterns in terms of color interplay as much as formal line, since the "line" is imposed by how the pieces are cut.

Modern painters have experimented with a similar form of construction. Early in this century,

Meadow Lily,
1974, 84" x 84"

several artists worked in the medium of collage, and toward the end of his career in the 1940s, painter Henri Matisse created a body of beautiful paper cutouts called *Jazz* that are widely reproduced. Those technical experiments by so-called "fine artists" resemble appliqué quilts—which happens to be one of the initial quilt construction techniques Michael employed.

Meadow Lily, Michael's first completed full-size quilt, shows the artist already restless with the limitations of traditional quilt design. Most of this quilt is pieced, although the stems and two leaves in each block are appliquéd. The hand-pieced block designs elaborate the rectangle-triangle into a number of trapezoids and the curved line of the leaf contrasts with the rigidly angular geometry of the other pieces. This same conflict of straight versus curved line continues in the quilting itself—rigorously diagonal within the pattern blocks, then almost mischievously curved in the border.

By 1975, when Michael created *Razzle-Dazzle* and *Bedloe's Island Pavement Quilt*, he tapped the Amish quilting tradition with the eye of a color-field artist. *Razzle-Dazzle* explores the relationship of separate visual planes as expressed by color. The color choices also hint how Michael will expand his color palette in the coming years. The trapezoid—really just a rectangle divided into parts and reassembled with a slant—again dominates. To ensure that the viewer doesn't miss the point, the bottom corners of the quilt are cut off. Michael says that these clipped corners were a response to the quilt's drape over the foot of the bed. But like most of Michael's work, *Razzle-Dazzle* is removed a step from its function as a quilt to take on the role of art displayed on a wall. The clipped corners are something of a visual joke—like telling the viewer to let her or his mind fill in the missing pieces.

Although by 1975 Michael had chosen to make almost all of his quilts by piecing rather than appliqué, the painterly parallels remain striking. *Bedloe's Island Pavement Quilt*, while clearly Amish in its design ancestry, is also a marvelous articulation of the late work of Piet Mondrian, a painter probably best known for the strict geometry of *Broadway Boogie-Woogie*, a painting of a grid with selected tiny squares colored in. The naturally hard edge of cut fabric lends itself well to this geometric branch of modern art, and *Bedloe's Island Pavement Quilt* could be seen as Michael's homage to an artistic forebear.

*Bedloe's Island
Pavement Quilt,*
1975, 76" x 84"

"In the early 1970s, after
I'd been interested in
traditional American
quiltmaking for a couple
of years, I learned about
the quilts of the Amish
and fell head-over-heels
in love with their mar-
riage of powerful and
often surprising color
combinations and simple
design structures. When
a friend passed along a
large box containing
small samples of men's
shirting and suiting
material, I was inspired
to use the great diversity
of colors I found in that
box in a quilt that
would emulate aspects
of the Amish quilts I so
admired at the time.
So *Bedloe's Island
Pavement Quilt* came
into existence. While it
reflects my own take on
color and my own twist
on simple four-patch
modules, it nevertheless
embodies a nod of the
head to those Amish
quiltmakers who didn't
shy from unusual color
pairings and uncommon
pattern arrangements."

"My formal art training has certainly INFLUENCED my thinking about what might happen on a quilt's SURFACE, but my study of the history of quilts and the METAMORPHOSIS of quilt patterns and design, especially of Amish quilts, has had an equivalent influence on the DEVELOPMENT of my work."

Elaborated Tangram,

1976, 94" x 94"

By 1976, when he completed *Elaborated Tangram* and *Tossed Salad Quilt*, Michael had taken the trapezoid about as far as it could go. With its exploration of ways to create the illusion of three dimensions by varying the background color, *Elaborated Tangram* amounts to a fabric parallel to some of the Op Art so hot in the New York art world at that time. *Tossed Salad Quilt* disturbs that rigorous geometry by fracturing space as if all the right angles were suddenly tossed askew—like a tossed salad. Different as they are, they represent complementary approaches to ways to define space.

The two quilts also show Michael working with an idea that's been floating around in modern art circles for a half century—that a form, even if it's an abstract form, acquires its own "personality." It becomes a symbol that has no direct translation—except that when the viewer looks at it, he or she sees an artist's hand at work. It's the central idea behind abstract art—something in a work of art can be beautiful, powerful, moving, or amusing in itself without having to refer to anything outside the art.

For all his attachment to such Big Ideas, Michael also feels a strong emotional pull from the homier, domestic quilting tradition. Behind all his elegant geometry, it always seems that he is on the verge of revealing an underlying organic form. In *Winter Cactus* we see the first of Michael's attempts to reconcile the domestic values of and references to the natural world so often found in traditional quilting with his determined intellectual exploration of form, space and color. The title alone is a giveaway—the shapes and colors evoke the humble windowsill houseplant. At the same time, he is beginning his exploration of curved lines by approximating them with angles—piling triangles upon trapezoids, approximating a curve by gradually reducing the angle.

Tossed Salad Quilt,
1976, 90" x 102"

Winter Cactus,

1978, 42" x 42"

Around 1976, Michael James began to question the necessity of hand-piecing. Once he made the decision to machine-piece some quilts, his production sped up, and with it, his ability to experiment.

Yet the seminal quilt from this period, *Night Sky 1*, is not pieced at all: It is quilted on whole fabric. As such, it marks Michael's most successful attempt up to that point at composing a quilt as a single broad composition rather than a construction of parts. The polished cotton, Prussian blue surface is meticulously quilted in a complex

of swirled patterns (shades of Vincent van Gogh's *Starry Night*) that evokes its title subject. It manages to express Michael's personality, yet at the same time it is exactingly geometric. This particular quilt salutes the quilting tradition with a master's example of stitchery—and bids adieu to the traditional geometry of quilting. It will be two decades before Michael revisits his quilting roots.

Night Sky I, 1977,
74" x 90"

PLANE

Night Sky II, 1977,
88" x 96"

The sequel, *Night Sky II*, employs the stitchery forms in a pieced quilt with the edges of pieces, in many cases, following the schematic laid out in *Night Sky 1*. This quilt signals a new direction in Michael's technique and his artistic goals. It is the first quilt in which he uses strips of fabric—in this case, curved strips. Moreover, it shows his

interest in exploring color transitions and shadings—a very painterly problem that is a lot harder to accomplish in pieced cloth. It also marks the second in what would become a series of quilts with a theme of "air and light," as artist David Hornung put it in the catalog essay for a 1983 retrospective exhibition of Michael's quilts at the Worcester Craft Center.

Night Sky II, detail
(whole quilt shown
on page 37)

"An important goal in my work continues to be the creation of VISUAL SURFACES in which the viewer can encounter UNEXPECTED color/space alliances and complex movements that will appear to have changed after multiple VIEWINGS. I want the viewer to DISCOVER new elements each time the object is seen and to feel that familiarity with it INTENSIFIES rather than diminishes each encounter."

Aurora, 1978,
96" x 108"

Other quilts intervened, but Michael returned to the series of "sky" quilts, including *Aurora*, *Moonshadow*, and *Dawn Nebula*, which create the illusion of space by using interlocking curves and colors that appear to be (but of course aren't) semitransparent overlays. These three quilts also depart from the two *Night Sky* quilts in their approach to the celestial subject matter. *Night Sky I* evokes the fabric of space—the background against which the stars shine. *Night Sky II*, with its glimmers of color, suggests objects against that background.

Moonshadow,
1979, 80" x 100"

Aurora, detail
(whole quilt shown
on page 40)

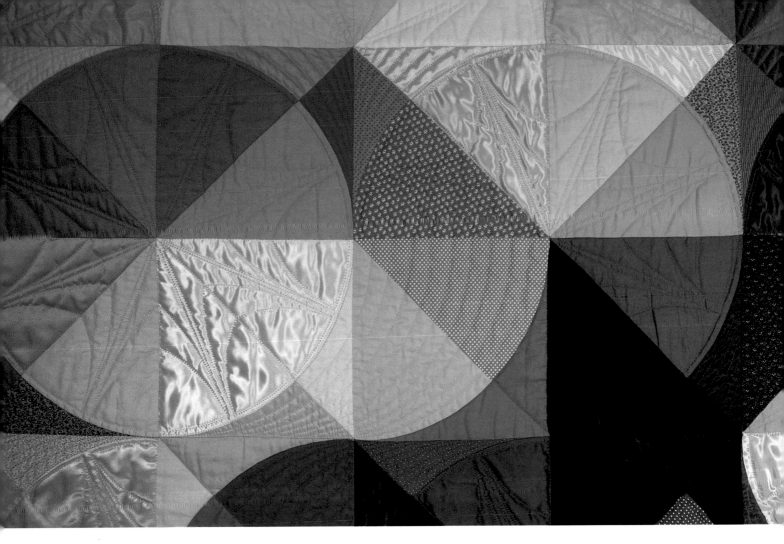

Moonshadow, detail
(whole quilt shown
on page 41)

43

THE ART OF MICHAEL JAMES

Dawn Nebula,
1979, 48" x 54"

But in *Aurora*, *Moonshadow* and *Dawn Nebula*, Michael tackles the problems of representing the transition between darkness and light. In *Aurora*, light itself is the figure against the background, whereas in *Moonshadow*, light is the background and darkness becomes the figure. The complexity of *Dawn Nebula* makes reading the figure-ground relationship more difficult, but Michael handles his symbolic representation of two kinds of light —sunrise and an exploding star—with flecks of bright color and carefully orchestrated transitions of hue.

Dawn Nebula, detail

As soon as Michael found he could create painterly color transitions in cloth, his next important quilt was a monochromatic piece that both recalled his celestial series and made a formal statement of the next world he was planning to conquer.

Suntreader: Monophony is a logical progression in form and content from his earlier quilts, yet it is radically different in its formal design. The *Suntreader* series makes a clean break from the external grid while proclaiming the problem of the internal one. By dispensing with the rectangular

nature of the quilt at a time when artists in various media were striving to "break the frame," Michael was reflecting one of the intellectual problems in the fine art world.

But with the *Suntreader* quilts he interprets that broader art world problem in a quilter's terms. He sees the quilt block as the technical device that gets in the way of "breaking the frame." And in these quilts, he also both makes fun of and pays homage to the vanishing-point perspective of the Renaissance in the quilted lines. The "curve" converges with others like railroad tracks disappearing in the infinity of space —or being consumed by the white fire of the sun. The color, of course, comes straight out of quilting tradition. *Suntreader: Monophony* is Michael's manifesto tacked on the door of the *White Quilt.*

The tension in this series grows directly from geometry as defined by frame (round), by stitch (curved and infinite), by block pattern (perpendicular), and, in *Suntreader No. 3,* by color (diagonal

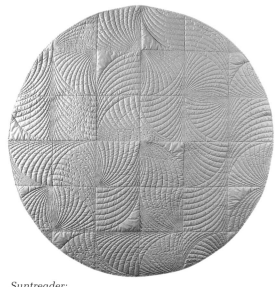

Suntreader:
Monophony, 1979,
60" diameter

RAINBOW

Suntreader No. 3,
1980, 60" diameter

Quintet, 1980,
68" x 68"

or transverse). Coming as the pivotal series between the celestial images, which have fairly direct references to the natural world, and the first of Michael's strip-pieced construction quilts, the *Suntreader* quilts are both "of this world" and unworldly. Their subject is the tension between the natural and the contrived—between the unordered chaos of the world outside our control and the patterns we try to place on that chaos to understand it.

By the end of the 1970s, Michael was working primarily in series of quilts, sometimes entirely in a single series, sometimes alternating between series. His next group—including *Quintet, Rhythmetron, Strip Quilt No. 5* and *Regatta*—marked a technical departure that allowed Michael to explore complicated color gradations while still allowing for visual "accidents" to occur in the studio. He has said that what he missed about painting were those "happy accidents" where a "mistake" could open up new possibilities.

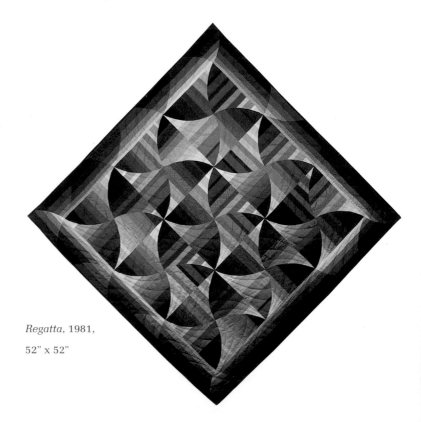

Regatta, 1981,
52" x 52"

"ART is a LANGUAGE: it takes part

of a LIFETIME to become fluent.

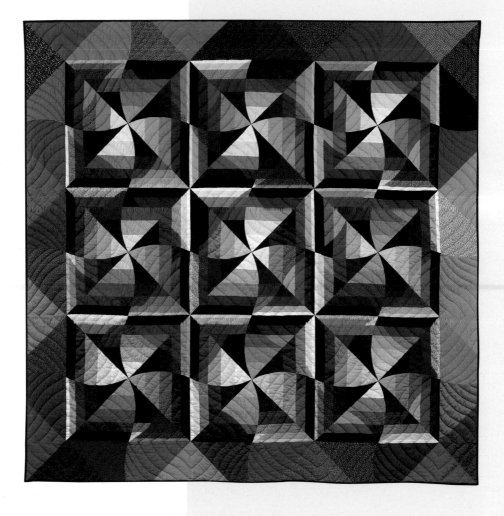

Rhythmetron, 1980,
68" x 68"

Don't however, expect everyone

to UNDERSTAND your dialect."

The Seasons, 1981,
174" x 54"

With this group Michael began to practice "strip-piecing" in a fashion that effectively created his own unique cloth. He would cut thin strips of colored fabric, then stitch them together in graduated hues or tones to create entirely new striped cloth. This "new" cloth would serve as the material for the quilt pieces. As a group, these quilts are a transitional phase in Michael's work: a playful investigation of the possibilities of strip-piecing combined with his experiments in using curved forms versus angular forms to create the illusion of space and volume and to create a vibrancy that would simulate movement.

About 1981, Michael made a decision that has been controversial in some quarters: to sew entirely by machine. On one hand, it was a logical extension of his work to that point. Strip-piecing virtually demanded the use of a sewing machine;

The Seasons, detail

as Michael observes, strip-piecing requires cutting across seams, and hand-sewn seams would unravel. And beginning with the *Interweave* series Michael decided to place his quilting "in the ditch," that is, in the seams between strips. This had the effect of making each piece more two-dimensional while de-emphasizing the three-dimensional "hand" of the cloth. It also made each piece less "quilt-like," if one considers decorative quilting an essential component of a traditional quilt. Admittedly, the argument about hand versus machine sewing was one of taste and identification with the handcraft tradition. Michael's hand-sewing was (and is) so meticulous that it is difficult to identify it as hand work. With the decision to minimize surface distraction, the necessity for handwork vanished.

De-emphasizing the contrast between the quilted surface and formal composition allowed Michael to explore the possibilities of color and brightness transitions inherent in his type of strip piecing. He could also more effectively mine the geometric potentials of this technique. *Interweave II* revisits a theme from the celestial series—a bright central field that fades, like a sunset or an aurora, as it edges off to darkness. Michael is unusually well read and curious, and in this quilt and the group that immediately follows, he plays with several natural phenomena from the world of physics. In *Interweave II*, he seems to be representing either the physical phenomenon of afterglow or the halo effect of light shining around an astronomical body (as the dark moon seems to have a halo around it during an eclipse).

Interweave 7, 1986,
60" x 60"

Interweave II,

1982, 68" x 68"

His next group of quilts make similar if obscure reference to natural phenomena. *La Tempête* evokes lightning by examining swirls of light playing, very much like a windstorm, through a stylized background of diagonal stripes and concentric diamond patterns. *Metamorphosis* and *Blue Undercurrents* feature many of the sine wave shapes (like the letter "S" turned on its side) of earlier series—here played against perpendicular stripes.

Metamorphosis,

1984, 84" x 84"

Blue Undercurrents,
1983, 70" x 70"

"The CURVED seam as a design form

offers literal FLUIDITY and an organic

FLEXIBILITY that cannot be achieved

with the straight seam. Curved seam

images have the capacity to pull us

more actively into and around the

quilt surface. They become more

SENSUAL designs."

By the time Michael concludes this series with *Air Structure* and *Air Structure 2*, his shapes and forms have become very intricate. But these worm-like stripes—reminiscent of the amoeba-shaped figures seen in the paintings of surrealists Joan Miró and Jean Arp—are a product of the strip-piecing. They are sine waves cut from darker fabric on a light ground. With an aspect ratio of 1:3, the *Air Structure* quilts also depart radically from traditional quilt form. Their dimensions— 15 feet by 5 feet—echo their purpose as architectural installations in large spaces. (Michael's quilts are a good fit with contemporary architecture, as their crisp lines complement the relatively stripped-down line of most newer buildings while the colors and sensual qualities of the fabric soften an otherwise impersonal environment.)

Air Structure,
1983, 180" x 60"

Air Structure 2,
1984, 174" x 58"

Air Structure 2

———

"My work has been intended for the wall because that's where it was created and that's where the imagery can be read most clearly; I had no objection to the use of quilts on beds, but I didn't believe that to be a necessary aspect of the nature of the quilt.

Quilts can have as much emotional resonance hung vertically as draped over the contours of the bed. Each state has its respective integrity, assuming the surface pattern and the material form respond to one another and to the intended audience."

In 1985, Michael began a series of quilts collectively called *Rhythm/Color* that he based on motifs from music and dance. A logical extension of the curving diagonals that dominate the *Air Structure* quilts, he begins to use curved forms to deliberately obscure the compositional grid on which he had designed his quilts from the beginning.

The grid is discernible as 10 x 10, but the quilts suggest certain dance forms that employ time signatures far more fluid. *Rhythm/Color: Spanish Dance* appears to use the sweepingly patterned areas of flamenco (in quartet form), while *Rhythm/Color: Morris Men* reflects the weaving pattern of that form of British folk dance.

Rhythm/Color: Morris Men, 1986, 100" x 100"

bye

Rhythm/Color:
Spanish Dance,
1985, 100" x 100"

Rhythm/Color:
Bacchanal, 1986,
73" x 73"

". . . the RHYTHMS in the pieces,

although they are visual (the stripes

and so on) are also based in MUSICAL

rhythms, consonances and dissonances,

that by some sort of OSMOSIS have

worked their way into the quilts."

The references had become less literal by the time Michael composed *Rhythm/Color: Bacchanal*, with its whirling figures and complex geometry on nine circles on the 10 x 10 grid. (The inspiration for this quilt was the *Bacchanale* sequence in Saint-Saëns' modern operatic composition, *Samson et Dalila*.) *Rhythm/Color: Improvisation 3* has left the comparatively simple rhythmic figures of folk dance behind in favor of a wave-like progression from jazz. Notably, this is a rare composition in that it "moves" from lower right to upper left.

Rhythm/Color: Improvisation 3, 1987, 102" x 102"

Zag-Edge 2, 1986,
50" x 50"

Zag-Edge 2

"Light holds fascina-
tion for the quiltmaker.
Suggesting the move-
ment of light across a
surface, or creating
the illusion of light
coming out from the
image, can be intriguing
involvements."

Bias Cut, 1986,
88" x 67"

Following the *Rhythm/Color* series, Michael
began to work with radical angles in the *Zag* suite
that includes *Zag-Edge, Zag-Edge 2* and *Bias Cut*
(all 1986). These particular quilts employ the
illusion of flat planes in three-dimensional space
to disguise and almost obliterate the grid. A close
examination of each quilt shows the 10 x 10 grid
(including the single block "border"), but the
complexity of composition distracts the eye
from that formal arrangement. Strong diagonals
play a part in the illusion, but the juxtaposition of
differing brightness levels determines the apparent planes.

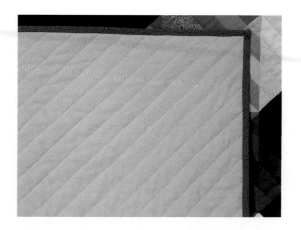

Bias Cut,
detail of back

Immediately following, Michael began to synthesize the lessons of the *Rhythm/Color* and *Zag* series with a small suite illustrated here by *Red Zinger*. He merges the diagonals of the *Zag* quilts with the curves of the *Rhythm/ Color* pieces, then deliberately violates the frame by including small segments that project beyond the box-like enclosures. The grid on which he has composed them has all but vanished. In a postscript to this

stage of dismantling the grid, Michael constructed *Neo-Geo* in 1987—a series of cloth panels (some strip-pieced, some not) in three dimensions. Certain panels actually overlap the others, and the grid has no traces at the surface. It is interesting to note that this quilt parallels a style

Neo-Geo, 1987,
58" x 43"

favored by many artists working in the media of wood, glass and jewelry in the late 1980s. This post-modernist pop style faded quickly and *Neo-Geo* is unique in Michael's work.

The radical forms of *Neo-Geo* find a parallel, however, in *Flying Buttress,* a quilt where Michael explores the visual tension between angular and curved forms. In terms of Michael's artistic development, this quilt is interesting because the abstract figure appears to float freely in space instead of being juxtaposed against a background. In this manner it foreshadows a series of quilts later in 1988 that break the smooth edges of the frame completely.

67

Double Image,
1987, 72" x 108"

Rain Dance, 1987,
57" x 57"

In *Double Image* and *Rain Dance*, Michael continues to explore different levels of planes and works with the contrast between curved and straight diagonals. The "forms," if they can be called that, seem to extend beyond the limits of the quilt edges into an imaginary infinity, defined both by light-like rays and wave-like ripples. In *Split Shift*, the frame is divided diagonally with angular forms on the upper left and curved forms on the lower right—sort of a preview of the *Cascade* series.

The *Cascade* quilts include *Cascade: Double Diagonal*, *Cascade 4*, *Red/Green Cascade* and *Double Cascade: Yang, Yin.* At first glance, they read as rippling waves superimposed on square planes within square planes. Again, Michael has suggested that the forms continue beyond the frame, implying the passage of time from memory (outside the frame) to present (the "snapshot") to future.

Double Image

"I want TWO THINGS for every piece that

I do: AESTHETIC and TECHNICAL integrity."

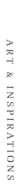

Cascade: Double
Diagonal, 1988,
57" x 57"

Cascade 4, 1989,

45" x 45"

"The hardest thing to CONTROL isn't

paint or thread or solder, but one's EGO."

Double Cascade:
Yang, Yin, 1989,
102" x 51"

Waves 2: Storm
Surge, 1988,
104" x 91"

Another group of quilts Michael was making at the same time, the *Shadowbox* series, opposes triangular forms with a strong diagonal thrust. Represented by *Zed Structure*, *Point/Counterpoint*, and *Transparent Shadowbox*, this series shows Michael examining ways to redivide the "box" of the quilt surface with diagonal sectioning. By playing the receding planes of ever-smaller boxes against the diagonal lines, he manages to create a vigorous—and shifting—perspective.

The Waves series, shown here as *Waves 1*, *Waves 2: Storm Surge* and *Waves III*, picks up some of these same concerns more literally with the idea of water as form. But two important changes also appear: Instead of lines that wave and swirl, Michael has introduced entire planes that appear to be in motion; and he has set aside the continuous edge of the traditional quilt. Michael's previous quilts were mostly square or rectangular, although he also made a few circular quilts. In either case, however, the integrity of the continuous frame held. The *Waves* series, however, violates that line to create a vivid sense of movement, as if the waveforms are rolling across the flat plane of an ocean surface.

Waves III, 1989,
45" x 58"

Waves I, 1988,
98" x 84"

Zed Structure,
1990, 63" x 63"

"Stripes allow me a STRAIGHTFORWARD

way to organize a broad color palette

that's COMPATIBLE with a standard

patchwork process, so that NEITHER

the stripe nor the process DOMINATES

the surface imagery."

Point/Counterpoint,
1989, 39.5" x 39"

*Transparent
Shadowbox,*
1988, 56" x 56"

Panorama: Konkordiaplatz 2, 1989, 141" x 51"

By 1989, Michael had succeeded in entirely obscuring the grid structure beneath his quilt compositions. In a very real sense, he is creating an art in fabric that is directly comparable to monumental abstraction in painting—imposing objects that do not represent or stand in for anything else. Yet at the same time, these pieces are clearly recognizable as quilts.

With the *Konkordiaplatz* group (1989-1990), which includes *From the Mountaintop*, *Panorama: Konkordiaplatz 1* and *2*, and *Aletsch*, Michael draws from the natural world. As he says, "These quilts represent efforts to synthesize my sensory responses to a particular space: the vast mountainous basin in the Swiss Alps that encloses the Aletsch glacier, the largest in Europe. In the summer of 1988 I spent several days hiking along its perimeter, which extends many kilometers from the Jungfrau firn. What impressed me most was the very audible sound of millions of gallons of water rushing unseen beneath the perfectly still expanse of glacier. It seemed incongruous: the unrelenting movement of so much water and the stony rigidity of so much ice." What a marvelous analogy to his own work!

Preliminary gouache maquette-in-progress for commission of *Panorama: Konkordiaplatz 1*

*From the
Mountaintop,*
1989, 90.5" x 68"

Aletsch, 1990,
83" x 41"

A strong, if sometimes hidden, affinity for the natural world runs through Michael James' quilt compositions, and the Aletsch glacier was a perfect metaphor for his struggle between solid, uncollapsing forms and liquidity of movement. Michael expresses his sense of awe for these great natural forces with a subtle art historical reference: The three-panel composition of these quilts is modeled on medieval and Renaissance altarpieces.

Panorama:
Konkordiaplatz 1

Panorama:

Konkordiaplatz 1,

1989, 150" x 50"

*Sky/Wind
Variations 2,*
1990, 86" x 51"

*Sky/Wind
Variations*, 1990,
144" x 72"

The lessons of the *Konkordiaplatz* group
reverberate in the quilts that immediately follow,
notably *Sky/Wind Variations*, *Sky/Wind Variations 2*
and *Expanded Force Field*. The composition of
Sky/Wind Variations in four individual panels both
echoes the altarpiece references of the
Konkordiaplatz group, and the four winds/four
directions tradition of a more pagan creed.

At the same time, Michael is casting back to
explore wave forms again—here the interlock of
crest and trough. *Expanded Force Field* examines
the energy from the other perspective—the
particle instead of the wave. While on one hand
the composition might be seen as harnessing
vectors, it also represents an interesting play of
form versus color. Although the composition can
be dissected as a series of interlocking right triangles, Michael uses color to lead the eye away
from closure of the form, creating a dynamic that
literally explodes—that is, it expands forcefully
toward (and, by implication, beyond) the frame.

*Sky/Wind
Variations*

"So, I look at one of my quilts and

when I SEE THROUGH the surface

image to the complex of stripes

supporting it, they are as many and

various and INTERCONNECTED as

lives lived in the here and now, and

in that sense they are a METAPHOR

for the COSMIC ORDER that governs

those lives being lived, that keeps

them from IMPLODING CHAOTICALLY."

Studio view with
Expanded Force Field

Basting *Expanded Force Field*

*Expanded Force
Field*, 1991,
79" x 79"

making idylls

Expanded Force Field represents a solution in Michael's work, at least for the time being, to handling angular forms. In 1992, Michael began a series that fuses his sophistication in representing curved forms and his elegant formalism with angles. In *Bourrée*, the first of the group, he limited the variations in curves to concentrate on working out the fusions of color from area to area. As such, it is the curved-line counterpart to *Expanded Force Field*. Michael says the title comes from a movement of Bach's third solo cello suite, and the interplay of form and tonality certainly suggests both the intricate formality of Bach and the mellow timbre of the cello.

In this series, Michael has let go entirely of the grid structure without calling attention to that achievement. (It is possible to superimpose a grid on many of these compositions, just as it is possible in analytical geometry to describe any curve. But a grid analysis is exactly that—an imposition, not a master plan.) Finding his way to freedom from geometry also seems to have sparked an intensely fertile period.

Lush Life is something of a turning point, since it both looks backward to Michael's fondness for forms that look like they come from nature and forward to his personal geometric vocabulary. A kind of joy seems to spring from the surface, as vigorous (and rather vegetable-like) forms exude an animal energy. The companion piece, *Hot Pursuit*, shares the vigor and the forms that imitate nature. But the surface overpowers the structure, making a space that seems rather intimate without the imposing structure of a grid.

Bourrée, 1992,

47" x 47"

"*Lush Life* refers to a sense of rich, verdant growth and energy, aspects of the Eden that this earth was once upon a time. The movement here is meant to be natural, vigorous, and spontaneous. The biomorphic nature of the forms emphasize the reference to the eco-sphere."

Some of the forms also make reference to the pointed curves seen in Asian landscapes and seascape art—the cresting waves of Japanese prints, the bamboo of Chinese brush paintings. This Orientalism is hardly a coincidence. The movement of forms in *Processional* is a direct reference to traditional Japanese court dance and pantomime.

Worktable view

Work-in-progress

Lush Life, 1992,

73" x 73"

Hot Pursuit, 1992,

46.5" x 46.5"

"My quilt surfaces often reflect my own emotional and psychological states, and with *Hot Pursuit* I was in fact feeling that sense of excitement and energy that accompanies a creative high, especially one experienced after the fallow period of little or limited discoveries. I was excited by the new way I had found to approach form in the quilt surface and felt that I was securely onto the scent of a much sought-after development in my work."

"North LIGHT is still best."

Processional,
1992, 118" x 68"

"In *Processional* the
intent was to reflect a
series of highly formal-
ized movements, such as
those that might define
a traditional Japanese
dance or pantomime.
Each visual gesture here
is dependent on the
sequences of tensions
and forces that exist
among the bracketing
and bracketed figures."

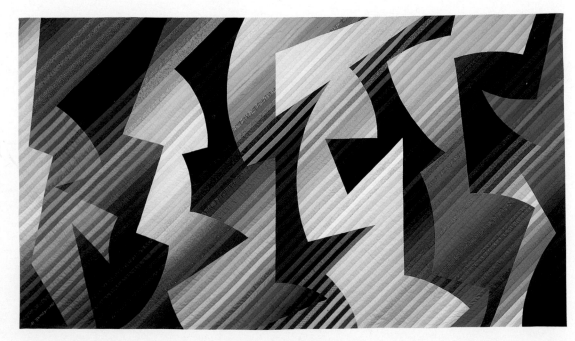

Vortex, 1993,
48" x 48"

shot of intricate dance-like movement. Compare the successor quilt, *Electric Boogie*, which plays with similar forms but which, by using a brighter background and more contrast, creates the illusion of active movement rather than a snapshot of motion. In *Electric Boogie* Michael's composition also draws the eye beyond the individual forms to a consideration of rhythms that he represents with bright patches in the upper left and lower

At the same time, Michael James the cool-headed and detached intellectual, shows a flip side as Michael James the sensualist. The forms of *Suspended Animation* directly echo those of *Processional*, but they are composed in a radically different way. Whereas *Processional* marches across the frame in a stately fashion, the curved and jagged forms of *Suspended Animation* form a dervish-like whirl of activity. Michael has said that he was trying to reproduce the "spontaneity of graffiti" with this work. He accomplished his goal.

The title of *Suspended Animation* is a clue to Michael's intention in this series of post-grid quilts. In fact, the activity does seem suspended—a snap-

Electric Boogie,
1993, 58" x 58"

Suspended Animation,
1992, 90" x 90"

"*Suspended Animation*
employs a labyrinthine
complex of curved and
jagged forms to manipu-
late the surface of the
piece, pushing and
pulling and twisting and
sliding in a kind of wild
free-for-all. Among other
things I was thinking of
the immediacy and
spontaneity of graffiti
and of its highly charged
energy. Electric boogie
meets patchwork."

right, separated by a diagonal band from lower
left to upper right. The off-center brightness of
the corner patches is like the syncopation of
boogie music, which takes the same musical
measure as a march but emphasizes the "off beat"
—a rhythm of "one TWO three FOUR" instead
of the steady "ONE two THREE four" of a march.

If there is one lesson in looking at Michael
James' career, however, it is that neither his intellectual nor his sensual impulse dominates for
very long. In *Vortex* he returns to an emphasis on
egg-shaped forms, piled up in layers of space like
slices from a cone. In contrast to the activity
implicit in the title, Michael creates a feeling of
tranquility and solidity, partly by using a soft and
subdued palette of colors.

Quilt No. 150
(Rehoboth
Meander), detail

"I read stripes as TIMELINES, visual

analogues to the PROGRESS of a

life: an inexorable MOVEMENT from

beginning to end."

*Quilt No. 150
(Rehoboth
Meander)*, 1993,
53" x 53.5"

Formalism appears even more explicitly in *Quilt No. 150 (Rehoboth Meander)* through an ordered arrangement of four columns and an exploration of Michael's peculiar forms as stand-ins for ideographs. The organization makes the quilt suggestive of a page of script written in columns—the way Chinese and Hebrew are written. The subsequent rectangular quilt *Out of Line* tumbles the forms, suggesting that the pair might be thought of as a duet—a before and after of meaning, or the monument and its equally beautiful ruins.

Between the two, Michael revisits his comb-shaped forms in *Full Circle*, one of two quilts that return to the circle for a different series of explorations than those in the *Suntreader* series a decade and a half earlier. *Full Circle* is what might be called an inhabited world—an active colony of forms swimming in close harmony beneath a circular membrane. *Roundabout*, on the other hand, gracefully combines the curved and triangular forms to suggest a convex view of the skin of the sphere.

Quilting *Out of Line*

Out of Line, 1994,
45.5" x 45.5"

Full Circle, 1993,
67.5" diameter

98

Roundabout, 1994,
77" diameter

starting
over

The quilts of 1992-94 capture the artist at the height of his form. He has effectively solved certain apparent limitations of the quilt form as an artistic medium—specifically the grid—and has, for a while, settled the conflict between lyric spontaneity and his own love of order. Rich in color, dynamic in form, playful in conception, they represent an artist who has fashioned a new order for his medium—the exploding joy of brushwork expressed with the modestly subordinated labor of pieced cloth.

While these 1992-94 quilts hardly represent a conclusion of Michael James' career, they are the beginning of the last suite of strip-pieced quilts. Although many people had come to see strip-piecing as his signature style, Michael felt that he had exhausted that particular approach and was finding it harder and harder to find something fresh to say with it.

Spirit Dance,
1994, 49.5" x 49.5"

Hot Spots, 1995,

54" x 54"

He was visiting the National Gallery in Oslo, Norway, when inspiration ambushed him. He had gone to see the museum's definitive collection of paintings and prints by Edvard Munch, the artist best known for *The Scream*, but a chance encounter with a different artistic tradition laid the groundwork for a radical shift in his own work. He wandered into a side gallery where the walls were covered with 16th and 17th century

Russian icons and he was struck by the vestments in some of the images—vestments modeled in strong geometric patterns.

The image that resonated most strongly for Michael was the St. Nicholas cross, a black and white pattern where figure and ground are perfectly complementary. His strong emotional response to the motif got him thinking about a new direction for his studio quilts. He re-examined traditional Amish quilts and found that he admired how their makers achieved powerful surfaces with very few shapes and colors. He felt ready to abandon the technical complexity of the strip-pieced quilts for a more direct approach.

Intersections,
1994, 55" x 55"

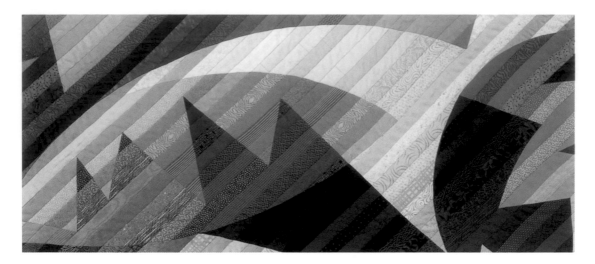

Protective Coloration,
detail

"Works completed
between 1992 and mid-
1996 were about various
tensions as well: the tension between the stripes/
strip-piecing process and
the surface imagery; the
tension between the
impulse toward order and
the potential for chaos;
the tension inherent in
metamorphosing forms
that were neither fully
geometric nor biomorphic.
Out of a system of parallel
stripes I attempted to
create a world of forms
and movements and
interactions that were as
many and varied as those
systems in nature, in
physics, and in music for
which they functioned as
visual analogues."

Earthly Pleasures,
1995, 65.5" square

Protective Coloration,

1995, 46" x 46"

Michael has done what artists often do when they make a stylistic transition—he has gone back to the design roots of his medium for inspiration. The post-*Ikon* pieces capitalize on some of the traditional strengths of the quilt. They exhibit a powerful geometry. They play with figure-ground relationships. They explore the effects of strong, primary colors.

The first quilt that took shape was *Ikon*, which was arranged as a triptych, or three panels, as some of his earlier quilts had been. In *Ikon*, Michael changed the crosses in the first panel into a reduced-contrast pattern in the second and finally fragmented them in the third panel. Michael saw many possibilities in the cross pattern —its repetitiveness, its ability to stand up to strong color, and the susceptibility of the simple forms to complex fracturing.

Michael found working on *Ikon* to be liberating, partly because he was approaching color and composition in a completely different manner than his work of the previous 15 years. In a sense,

Ikon, 1996, 74" x 79"

Sound and Fury,
1996, 84" x 55"

Yellow Brick Road,

detail

Michael has always been a master colorist—a talent that was essential in the strip quilts, where some pieces used literally hundreds of colors and hues. Now he is limiting the number of colors and feels that he is composing directly with color. That is, each form within the quilt is defined by the limits of a color rather than by a compositional line. In *Yellow Brick Road* and *Sound and Fury*, he explores the possibilities of a limited palette with the abandon of a painter who suddenly tries collage.

Yellow Brick Road also takes apart the St. Nicholas cross in the fashion that Michael used in the third panel of *Ikon*, but here he introduces a mustard color in place of stark white. The composition is still just two colors, but by reducing the contrast, he softens the edges while simultaneously calling attention to the "yellow" and its significance. Even the title carries a double edge, suggesting both the fantasy path of Oz and the resemblance to brick masonry in the compositional construction.

In *Sound and Fury*, Michael is using color to present a less ambiguous figure-ground relationship—almost as if he were flirting with pictorial representation. Actually, the composition has many of the hallmarks of a landscape painting—in this case suggested by the raised horizon line where the orange patches interact. The olive and blue forms suggest a foreground receding to background.

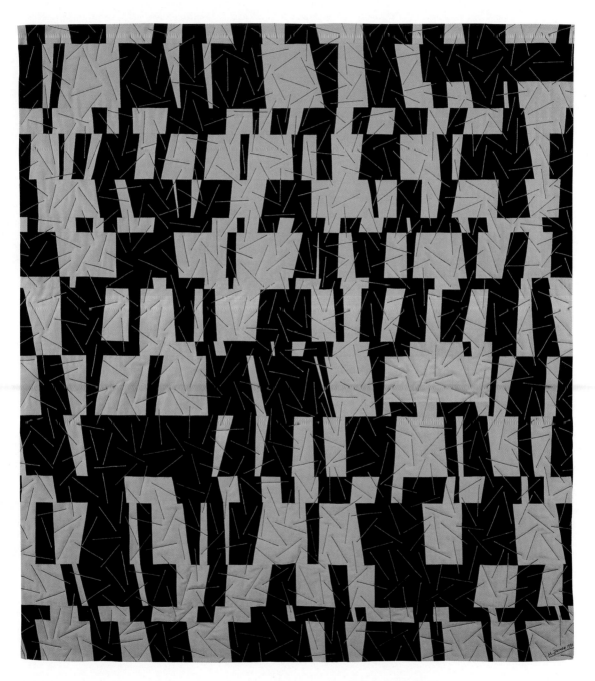

Yellow Brick Road,

1996, 72" x 88.5"

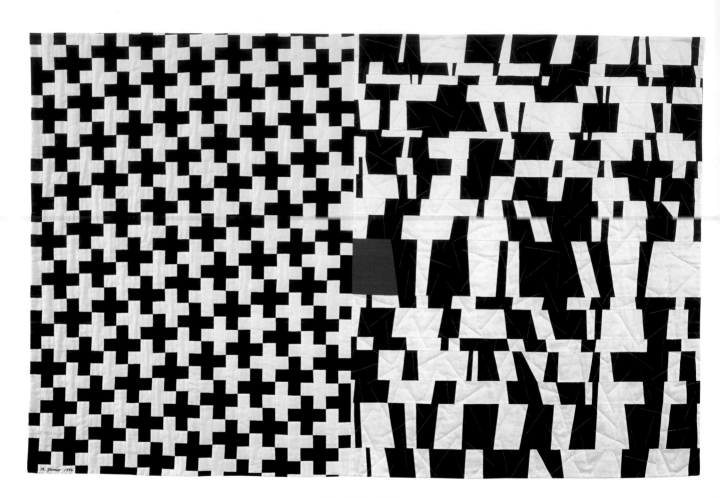

Crash Site, 1996,

76.5" x 50"

". . .the process allows me to start

from SQUARE ONE and build through to

a final product, all with the activity

of my own HANDS and my own MIND;

because I like to sew, PURE and SIMPLE;

because I like the substances of tex-

tiles, their weave and texture and the

way they hold COLOR."

Crash Site, detail
(whole quilt shown
on page 110)

Parallel Conversations,
detail (whole quilt
shown on page 115)

THE ART OF MICHAEL JAMES

In *Crash Site*, Michael uses the power of a single patch of red to disrupt an otherwise placid field of black and white. The title gives away what is already obvious—that the explosive red marks the border between orderly rows of crosses and the same crosses after they have been wrecked.

Michael's longstanding interest in surface embellishment shows up again in this new work, where a simplified composition seems to demand it. Michael uses quilting—even hand-quilting and, in the case of *Sound and Fury*, some embroidery —to elaborate the surfaces.

At the same time, he also re-evaluated his choice of fabrics and turned away from the cottons he had used so extensively in the past to wools, particularly wool challis, which he feels offer deeper colors and a richer feel and drape.

Because he limits the number of colors so strictly in these quilts, each color assumes heightened significance. Michael usually visualizes what he wants, and then he searches high and low for the right fabric. Interestingly, he has also begun to explore the possibility of strong, sometimes even jolting, color pairings, perhaps best illustrated in *Parallel Conversations*. In a sense, Michael felt that his quilts had become so serene and soothing that they were otherworldly—and he wanted to bring the discord of real life into his work.

Studio view

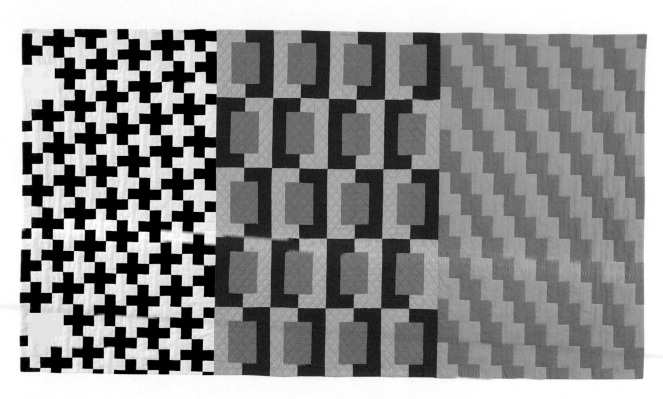

Parallel Conversations,
1997, 86" x 48"

"Recently I've gone back
to looking at Amish
quilts once again, to see
what I can learn anew
from them. *Parallel
Conversations* is the
result of a desire to sim-
plify by reducing my
color palettes and
streamlining the con-
struction process,
which in my final strip

quilts had become
extremely complicated.
Here I juxtaposed three
autonomous panels;
seven colors altogether,
including black and
white, presented so that
each brings out the best
in its companion(s). To
me, that's the essence of
what the Amish, at their
best, succeeded in doing
in their own quilts."

Michael knows that anyone who has followed his work will find the new quilts radically different. But the hallmark of his career is not any particular technique, but rather a willingness to respond to his creative impulses and follow them as far as they go. Sometimes a "style" will last a year or two, sometimes a decade and a half. Michael says that he never set out to have a signature style.

"All I want to do," he says, "is to respond to my artistic and creative impulses."

—*Patricia Harris and David Lyon*
© 1995, 1998 by Patricia Harris & David Lyon

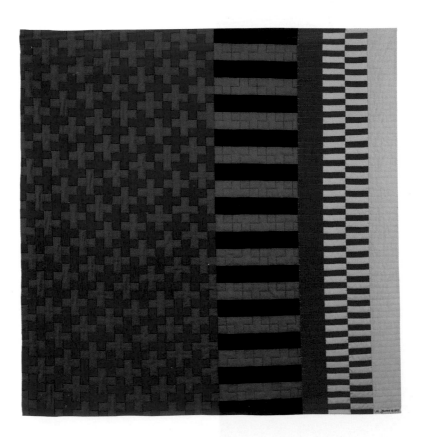

Zipper, 1997, 65" x 66.5"

"If I can offer any practical ADVICE

today to someone who wants to pursue

quilts as a studio art activity, I would

say simply: 'DO THE WORK.' Just do it.

. . . so, making has to be the priority,

and the energies of the artist's MIND

and HEART and HANDS have to be con-

centrated on the materials and the

processes that OCCUPY and ENLIVEN

the studio or workshop."

michael james:

"There are LIMITLESS possibilities, so

no one can tell someone else which

ROUTE is best. Every quilter has to

map her or his own DIRECTION."

view

an interview

Patricia Malarcher: How did you come to realize that, in quilts, you had found your own voice?

Michael James: It was a gradual process. To be honest, it seems that it's only in the last six or seven years that I've found it. The first thirteen of fourteen years were really a period of searching after who I was artistically. I did know, early on, that it was with quilts that I wanted to develop a life's work, because there I had found a marriage of me and the materials more compelling than with paint and brushes and canvas.

PM: Would you speak about the difference between making quilts and working with paint?

MJ: There are huge differences. The primary one is the insistent, process-oriented, step-by-step nature of building a quilt, starting with pieces

A and B and building on those systematically, doing certain things in a certain order. In painting you can put diverse materials together in random order and build in a less constrained way. I related better to an orderly kind of construction than to the open-ended possibilities that working on a canvas offered.

PM: The way you describe it, your work seems allied to architecture.

MJ: For a while, I considered the possibility of studying architecture, but I went into painting because something in me sought the kind of freedom that painting represents. Despite the limitations I've described in relation to quilts, I have experienced a sense of liberation—an experience that a painter might identify with—in making them. I feel that I've been able to rise over those limitations, and that it's been an exciting challenge to do so.

PM: Looking at slides of your work, from the earliest to the most recent pieces, I was aware of a progression from a unit-by-unit construction in an obvious grid to compositions with an overall flow that seem to reclaim the space of a painter.

MJ: I think I made a breakthrough a couple of years ago, one that I'd been aiming toward for seven or eight years, allowing me to leave behind the understructure. The traditional notion of what a quilt was had imposed the grid on my work as it has on that of most people making quilts over the last twenty years. At first I was comfortable with the grid, and it served my purposes, but I got to the point where I began to see it as a kind of prison. It became a necessity to break away from it. Then I did a series in which, although you couldn't see a literal grid on the surface, there was an underlying grid that supported what was on the surface. Finally, two years ago I eliminated the underlying grid; that opened up a huge range of possibilities.

PM: Did that breakthrough happen during your residency at the Chateau de La Napoule?

MJ: It was definitely tied to having had the residency, because it was there that I went back to working on paper and working primarily with oil-based pastels and crayons for the first time in nearly twenty years. That way of working was so different from the processes in which I had immersed myself; it reminded me that there was a whole other way of working and creating images. My focus had been so concentrated that I hadn't allowed room for that kind of experimentation. It also reminded me of the importance of play, especially play with unconventional materials or with materials that aren't the stuff with which an artist usually works. Out of that period came a number of drawings, which, although not quilt-like, embodied images that I eventually recognized as relevant to the types of fabric surfaces that I'd been creating. I started a series of quilts in 1992 whose roots are in several of those drawings; they were the first that completely abandoned the underlying grid.

PM: In choosing the quilt as your form of expression, did you consider that you would have to confront different issues surrounding the work such as the question of art versus craft, or the fact of being a minority male in a dominantly female world?

MJ: I certainly thought of both of those things. As for the question of art versus craft, I'll say that for myself personally, it's not an issue. I see many quilts, including some of my own, that are fully as artful as many paintings, sculptures, or objects that one would regard as conventional fine art forms. The work of one's hands and mind in producing an object is the same from medium to medium. I don't think there's a significant difference, although there might be a difference in terms of intent.

PM: What do you mean?

MJ: Well, if I decide to make a quilt, and open a book to look for a pattern, and decide to make a Bear's Paw pattern for my queen-size bed, and end up with an object that is 90 inches by 100 inches and drapes well over the sides of the bed and covers the pillows when the bed is made and provides warmth at night when the bed isn't made, and provides decorative interest to the room by virtue of its pattern, and is the result of hundreds of hours of careful stitching and attention to process, I don't think I've necessarily created a work of art.

PM: What have you created?

MJ: I've created a bed quilt, an object for use. Now if I decide to make a quilt that's 90 by 100 inches, and is a configuration of forms and colors, materials and techniques which, as a whole, give realization to some image that comes out of my own experience and thought processes and feelings about art and design and pattern as well as the notion of what quilts are or have been or can be, and that may work on a bed but doesn't have to in order to be understood, the odds are better that I will have produced something that might be considered art. I may not do that every time, but that's true of any artist.

PM: Could you define the difference between art, craft, and design?

MJ: Art is a state, a situation that a work enters when its expressive, symbolic, metaphorical, and/or decorative value assumes a communicative power that transcends its materiality. To me, craft is the process, the construction, the technical aspect of producing some object. To a degree, design is technical also, but whereas craft is focused on the construction end of the object, design is focused on the composition—essentially, on the interweaving of the surface elements—line, color, form, shape, etc.

PM: Would you say that design is concerned with both functional and aesthetic ends?

MJ: Yes, depending on what you're designing. If you're designing a piece of furniture, you have to be concerned about functional aspects. But you don't have to think functionally in terms of quilts, at least not in regard to studio quilts or art quilts. Most of them are thought of in the same terms as painting: something to go on a wall, with a decorative or communicative purpose—that is its function.

PM: But what is it that pushes good design and good craft into art?

MJ: All I can say is that there's something intangible embodied in a work of art that has the capacity to draw emotional and psychological responses from someone who encounters it. Most objects that are purely functional don't have that intangible quality.

PM: Beyond craftsmanship and design, art today is regarded as something that holds a mirror up to a particular culture and talks back to it in ways that are often confrontational. Where do you see your work in such a milieu?

MJ: I don't see that my work really fits in with what's going on in the art world today. It seems to fit in with what is going on in the studio craft movement. What I've said regarding quilts could be said about any studio craft medium like glass, furniture, ceramics, or other textiles. None of those really fit in with the currents of avant-garde art.

PM: Is the choice of making work that is harmonious rather than disturbing an escape from the real world?

MJ: When I'm in my studio I don't think in those terms but I can say this about my work: I'm by nature a very ordered person who depends on and likes a fair amount of structure in my life. Perhaps one reason I turned to quilts is because of the order that is imposed on process. The type of quilts that I make is a reflection of the type of person I am. That brings to mind the issue of stripes. I've been working with stripes for the last twelve or thirteen years. There's something about the regularity and the consistency that appeals to me, that I relate to, that gives me pleasure and satisfaction. Stripes are universal and elemental forms, archetypes in a way.

PM: Do you feel that by creating stripes in a physical way from fabric rather than by drawing or painting them on a surface, you are asserting their essence more emphatically?

MJ: Exactly. I'm not just making a flattened representation of a stripe, but I'm actually cutting the stripe and then putting many of these stripes together to make panels that become multicolored strip surfaces or expanses. It's a lot more labor-intensive to cut and sew stripes than it is to paint stripes. But it's never crossed my mind to paint the images I'm doing in fabric. If I were going to paint I would do something else.

PM: Although you might use 150 colors in the stripes of a quilt, there is a certain quality of light in your color that is uniquely yours. Is that intended?

MJ: When I'm doing the construction of the strip panels, which is a prelude to the actual creation of a quilt surface, I first choose the colors of fabric which will later be cut up into strips and then sewn into large panels. I choose 36 colors, on average, for each panel, usually without a particular reference to anything external to the color itself. I do decide occasionally, when I'm

running low on them, that I need to make very light runs of color in my panels, or runs that are warm or bluish or whatever. This is not done with any thought of creating a particular light effect later, but to fill in a gap in the color palette. Obviously, in a lot of my work the issue of light and space has been a concern and in composing many pieces I deliberately focused on them. But that was an afterword, if you will, to the composition of the stripes themselves.

PM: After you've made these panels and put a piece together, do you ever have a sense of connecting with something outside the work?

MJ: Sometimes when I start composing a piece on the wall I start to make associations with some natural or emotional reference, but my work is essentially abstract. There's very little in the whole body of my work that could be construed as representational although there are some pieces that have a representational aspect.

". . .I don't care if you call it out-

sider art, or insider art, or main-

stream art, or OUT-IN-LEFT-FIELD art, or

whatever. . .at least within the dis-

cipline it's important that some of us

go on pushing FORWARD and BEYOND

the past, the traditions. . .and all

the EXPOSURES I open myself up to

are only going to help me do that."

*The Metaphysics
of Action*, 1994,
101" x 101"

PM: What about the shapes suggestive of biomorphic forms in your newest pieces?

MJ: I can't say that I went about looking for biomorphic forms, but the forms that started to happen had a biomorphic quality. I make a particular shape, and step back and think, 'Oh, that shape looks like a leaf, or is starting to look like a flower or whatever.' It's not done with any intent, but is the shape that results from an effort to organize the space of the surface. It's an intuitive way to work, and is not often governed by some fixed idea of what I want to express or represent.

PM: Let's go back to your being among a male minority in the quilt field.

MJ: I did wonder, when I first got involved in quilts, what people would think of a man getting this serious and this focused on something that men, except for a handful, simply didn't do. I came to the conclusion that I had to do what I felt would feed me regardless of what anybody thought.

PM: Has being in a minority been advantageous?

MJ: Any minority attracts a certain amount of attention as a novelty, but I have always felt that the novelty of my gender in this medium wasn't enough to sustain interest in my work—the work itself had to speak and its construction had to be as rock-solid as any around. I think that has had more to do with the response that my work has received than the fact that I'm a man doing it. With all the discussion and theorizing that's gone on about gender roles in recent years, including the push against the dominant white male in contemporary society, I have felt somewhat uncomfortable when I've been put in a position of authority. I've juried shows, written catalogues, reviewed shows and books and so on related to the quilt world. So by virtue of my straight, conventional, late 1960s—early 1970s fine arts education, I could be perceived as a white male 'establishment' voice in a field that is 99% female. Certainly, some individuals are hostile to that male voice. Yet, I feel that my convictions about the validity of this medium relative to other media is proof of my commitment to quilts and quiltmaking and quiltmakers.

PM: Let's shift gears. You've mentioned Charles Sheeler as an influence; how is this reflected in your work?

MJ: I've been a longtime admirer of Charles Sheeler and a number of other Precisionist painters of the 1920s and 1930s, but I can't say they've actually influenced my work. Certainly, I've been attracted to that type of work, and have drawn from it an analogy with the type of work that I do, because I see it as precisionist.

PM: It's often said that people in craft mediums tend to take ideas that have already been developed in other fields, and simply rework them in different materials. It seems that when Sheeler and his contemporaries were working, they were expressing this in paint. Today, that's not a primary interest in painting, but your work still seems to reflect it. How would you answer someone who saw in your work a recycling of someone else's color theory into your own materials?

MJ: At this point, I don't think that my own way of handling color and of dealing with light and space and so on is derivative of any particular artist or style. If I were to feel that everything I did was derivative, then there'd be no reason to do it.

". . .I'm frustrated by a SENSIBILITY

that says I can't be trusted, that

my MOTIVES are open to question,

because of my GENDER."

PM: Let's talk more about these images coming into your work. They seem ambiguous, rather than specific. Do you think of them as metaphorical?

MJ: The free-form images I'm currently working with were foreshadowed by the drawings that I did in the fall of 1990, but when I did them I had no idea of what I wanted them to represent.

PM: Were you drawing from nature, or imagination?

MJ: I was drawing out of experience, and I was using drawing, as I use the designing of my quilt surfaces, as a way to swim in the world of color and form, to revel in the beauty of pure color and pure form. Essentially it's a reflection of an Abstract Expressionist approach to surface design. And, saying that, I realize that it's passé in relation to how people are thinking about artmaking today.

PM: You've spoken of having been trained in an Abstract Expressionist mode. Are there particular artists from the Abstract Expressionist school that have influenced you?

MJ: Are you asking whether my imagery reflects elements in other artists' work?

PM: Not necessarily; one can also be influenced by an artist's philosophy or an idea about what art is.

MJ: In that case I would say that hundreds of artists have influenced my work. I have made a point to learn about artists' lives through biographies or autobiographies, as well as artists' writings and commentaries on their work or on movements they've been involved in and so on. When an observer discusses my work, he'll often see the influence of Frank Stella—his name comes up a lot, of course, because in the 1960s Stella was doing his stripes and the compass curves and the protractor series. But from my vantage point, those have been the least influential among Stella's works; what have had more of an impact on me have been the aluminum, free-form constructions. Maybe in those there was a clue to understanding how I could develop form that would go beyond the grid substructure. I've looked at a lot of work by artists who would be thought of as colorists. David Hockney comes to mind. I don't look at my work and think of David Hockney, and I don't think many people would, but I think that his work has influenced mine. Matisse is another, but of course Matisse influenced Hockney, as Picasso did. The question of influences is very complex.

PM: Sometimes, influence can be subliminal, unrecognized until work is completed.

MJ: Well, the range of artists that I've looked at and absorbed through their work goes from the people we just spoke about to people like Bridget Riley, Francis Bacon, Brice Marden, Frida Kahlo, Andy Goldsworthy—I'm naming artists whose work is very divergent and who cover a broad range of styles, just to make the point. My work has also been influenced by my study of Amish quilts and other textiles including African fabrics and Central and South American weaving. And I don't want to overlook the influence that the work of other studio craft artists has had on my own. The glass artist, Dale Chilhuly, for example, and Diane Itter, who made absolutely incredible hand-knotted constructions, have both affected my work.

PM: What about artists who focused on color, like Josef Albers or Richard Anuszkiewicz?

MJ: Anyone who went through art school in the 1960s studied Albers so I'm certainly cognizant of everything he stood for. So yes, Albers has influenced my work, as well as Anuszkiewicz and the color Op Art stuff of the 1960s and 1970s. But what's influenced me more than their actual pieces has been what these people have said about their work.

PM: Could you give an example?

MJ: Well, for instance, Bridget Riley, in a catalogue essay, spoke about light and space and seeking a way to give visual form to an experience of a particular type of light at a particular moment of the day under particular climatic conditions. That idea speaks to me in a way that some of her paintings don't; perhaps she didn't succeed at doing what she set out to do because it was so elusive.

PM: Could you cite another example?

MJ: Well, Frida Kahlo, but again it's less a matter of the work itself being an influence. With her, it's a way of approaching the world, of being, in terms of the world. It's a sense of utter honesty and a kind of self-assuredness and self-awareness in the face of a large measure of —how do I express it?— inadequate attention?

Michael James
with son Trevor

"An important, if sad, REALITY of the art

world is that many artists never receive

the attention or the recognition that

their work deserves. So if that's what

your GOAL is, be prepared for frustra-

tion and disappointment. I think it's

WISER to put your mental and physical

energies into the WORK ITSELF. It's a

BETTER INVESTMENT and is more likely

to pay dividends in the long run."

PM: Do you mean that she knew she was a better artist than people gave her credit for being?

MJ: Exactly, and the fact that she knew she wasn't getting the attention she deserved didn't dissuade her in any way. She continued, despite great odds, to do what she knew she had to do. That's the type of thing that will influence me. It's what motivates me to continue doing what I do.

PM: How do you view the critically acclaimed fabric works of Lucas Samaras?

MJ: I was really energized by those fabric constructions he did back in the late 1970s and early 1980s. I came to New York to see those pieces in shows at the Pace Gallery and I also saw a collection at the Chicago Art Institute. Hilton Kramer did a long review of those pieces in the *New York Times*. He made reference to a resurgence of interest in patchwork and quilts but said Samaras was the only person to do anything original with it. Looking back, I think I now agree with him although I didn't then. However, I think that since then original work has been done in the fabrics medium by people who weren't tied into the New York art world. I actually saw Samaras' things more as paintings than as quilts. In fact, they were pieced fabric constructions that were stretched on stretcher frames; he never pretended to be making quilts.

PM: Today, a big issue in the art world is the intellectual content in the work. Would you say that, for you, the content is in the formal qualities?

MJ: There's no doubt that it's largely in the formal qualities. I've chosen not to put any kind of weighty sociological message in my work. It's just not what the work is about, and I'll never pretend that it is.

PM: Do you have a weighty philosophical reason for not doing so?

MJ: I suppose it's partly an impulse that has always been strong not to jump on the bandwagon; I haven't felt the need to. I've looked at the world, let's say, with a sense of awe. I've been attracted by what is harmonious and what is beautiful in the physical world, and I think my work has always been an attempt to synthesize my response to that. Now, certainly if I walk out the door of this building onto West 23rd St., within a block I'm going to encounter half a dozen homeless people begging for money. It's outrageous that our society is incapable of

PM: Let's go back to your use of stripes, which you called "archetypal." Since archetypes are rooted in universal human experience, could you relate the striped structure to some specific kind of experience?

MJ: Ultimately, I see the stripe as a kind of timeline. A stripe for me is like the line of somebody's life.

PM: Do you mean that is represents continuity?

MJ: I guess it's a symbol for order; I think that searching after order is an elemental drive even though nature may seem to conspire against that. It's also the elemental, rhythmic patterning, the plus and minus, yin and yang quality to the composition of a field of stripes that appeals to me.

PM: Your reference to rhythmic patterning reminds me of something we haven't yet talked about: you once mentioned that music has been important in the development of your work.

MJ: I work in my studio with music as a complement to whatever I'm doing. I know that when I'm building a piece on the wall and making decisions about forms and colors and placement and tensions and movements and all of that, I'm subconsciously reacting to the music that I'm hearing or that I've been listening to in the days or weeks leading up to that particular work.

providing its inhabitants with the things they need. But I don't feel any impulse to go back to my studio and make a quilt about homelessness or about societal inequities or injustices. It's not that I think that type of work can't be important and compelling —some of it is—but it's not what I'm interested in reflecting in my work.

PM: Could it be that in committing yourself to that which is harmonious and orderly, qualities which may have a kind of soothing value that is lacking in the world at large, you are helping to introduce or inject a sort of balance into the world?

MJ: I know this is true because people have told me that my work gives them a means to escape the oppressive realities that surround most of us on a daily basis. In that sense, my quilts function as metaphors for a perfect world. That's what they are for me. I can't control the world around me, but I can control color and form and fabric in my work; it's my only means of approaching perfection or harmony.

So, while the rhythms in the pieces are visual, they also are based on musical rhythms which by some sort of osmosis work their way into the quilts. I've always felt that visual surfaces could function as analogs to particular pieces of music; when I'm thinking about things that are happening in the surface of a quilt, I think of terms like timbre and brilliance and dissonance. I think of a run of colors or an interplay of colored stripes in a particular sequence as a segue from one area to another, or as an arpeggio or whatever, depending on what's going on.

PM: You were speaking of Frida Kahlo, and the fact that you could empathize with her persistence in spite of inadequate attention. Yet, you yourself have attained a level of success that, among artists, is above average. You've been able to survive on your art, to support a family, to travel.

MJ: You talk about a certain measure of success and recognition but that has been in a fairly small arena. The quilt world itself is a pond, and that is where most of my recognition has come from. The craft world, the fine craft world, is a small lake perhaps, and a certain measure of recognition has come from there. Then there's the ocean, certainly the great lake, that is the art world, and where does what I do fit into that?

PM: Does that bother you?

MJ: No, it doesn't bother me. I hope that a hundred years from now some of this work will still have the capacity to affect someone, but that's not why I'm doing it.

PM: At this point in your career, are you aware of any acquired wisdom, or insight, realized through the process of working?

MJ: I guess it would be that ultimately you're the only person that you have to answer to. If you respond to others rather than responding to yourself, the idea of producing work with integrity will remain elusive; you'll never do it. The only way you can produce work that has integrity is by turning inward and acknowledging the truth of who you are as a person and of establishing what your relationship to the process of artmaking is, or what you want it to be, and then working toward that. Despite what anyone else brings to your work you're the ultimate judge, and you have to be loyal to that inner voice that is the best guide that you're likely to have. Certainly other people can help, but other people can also trip you up. So finally you answer to yourself, and I think ultimately that's where integrity comes from. 'Know thyself'—it sounds simplistic, but essentially that's what it is.

Patricia Malarcher
This interview was recorded in New York City in January, 1994.

State of Mind, detail
(whole quilt shown
on page 133)

"The PAST does not condition my

work; I see a PLACE for a more for-

malistic APPROACH to quiltmaking."

biography

1949

Born in New Bedford, Massachusetts, June 30. Oldest of seven children of Robert A. James, Jr. and Claire C. (Savoie) James. English and French Canadian heritage.

1951-1967

Elementary and secondary education at St. Anthony's School, New Bedford. At the time, this was a bilingual (French/English) parish school.

1967-1971

Fine art studies at Southeastern Massachusetts University, North Dartmouth. Concentrations in painting and print-making. Studies color with Donald Krueger.
Initial interest in quilts begins sometime in 1970 with purchase of Dover Books editions of *One Hundred and One Patchwork Patterns* and *The Standard Book of Quilt Making and Collecting*.

1971

Receives Bachelor of Fine Arts Degree.
Moves to Rochester, New York and begins graduate studies in painting and printmaking at Rochester Institute of Technology. Works principally with non-figurative imagery realized in washes of acrylic stain on unprimed canvas, and multiple print editions in serigraphy. Interest in Native American culture provides a source for visual forms and themes in both painting and prints.

1972

Marries Judith A. Dionne.
Birth of son, Trevor Dionne James.
Begins making small quilts and patchwork items; largely self-taught.

1973

Receives Master of Fine Arts Degree.
By late summer 1973 has stopped painting in favor of quilt-making.
Does extensive research into quilt history and technique.

1974

In early 1974, attends lecture by Jonathan Holstein at Memorial Art Gallery of the University of Rochester. First exposure to actual Amish quilts.
Moves with his family to Somerset, Massachusetts. Occupies a four room apartment in which a part of the living room space serves as a studio.
In early autumn begins teaching art part-time at St. Anthony High School in New Bedford, substituting for his former high school art teacher.
Begins teaching adult education workshops in quiltmaking throughout southeastern New England.

1975

While teaching at the DeCordova Museum School, participates in the museum's exhibition *Bed and Board: Quilts and Woodwork*, one of the first large-scale exhibitions featuring non-traditional quilts.
Participates in *Quilts for '76* in the Cyclorama Building of the Boston Center for the Arts.

1976

Attends the first major quilt conference and exhibition held in Ithaca, New York and meets Beth and Jeffrey Gutcheon, Jean Ray Laury, and Myron and Patsy Orlofsky, all leading writers on quilts and quiltmaking.

1977

Begins extensive travel in the U.S. and Canada teaching and lecturing on quiltmaking, quilt design, and historical and contemporary quilts.
First solo exhibition of quilts, at Bridgewater (MA.) State College includes *Night Sky I*, *Razzle Dazzle*, *Elaborated Tangram*, and *Tossed Salad*, among others.
Night Sky II is selected for inclusion in exhibition *Young Americans: Wood, Plastic, Fiber, Leather* at the Museum of Contemporary Crafts in New York City.
Asked by Prentice-Hall, Inc., of Englewood, New Jersey, through the intermediary of the DeCordova Museum, to write a book on quiltmaking for their Spectrum Books Creative Handcraft Series.

1978

Participates in the jurying of the first Quilt National exhibition in Athens, Ohio. First book, *The Quiltmaker's Handbook: A Guide to Design and Construction*, is published by Prentice-Hall, Inc. Awarded a Visual Artist Fellowship in Crafts by the National Endowment for the Arts. Begins construction of a home/studio in Somerset Village.

1979

Awarded an Artist's Fellowship by the Boston Artists Foundation.
Moves into new home/studio, more than tripling his available workspace.

1980

First trip to England, in May and June, for lecture and workshop tour.

1981

Second book, *The Second Quiltmaker's Handbook: Creative Approaches to Contemporary Quilt Design* is published by Prentice-Hall, Inc.
Completes first corporate commission, *The Seasons* for the Waltham Federal Savings and Loan Association in Waltham, Massachusetts.
Begins first series of strip-pieced quilts.

1982

Exhibits *Interweave II* in exhibition *Pattern* at the American Craft Museum, NYC.

1983

First trip to France and Switzerland. Lectures in Paris and in Neuchâtel.
Ten-year retrospective *Michael James: Quiltmaker* takes place in October and November at the Worcester (MA) Craft Center.
Organizes concurrent group exhibition *Fabric Constructions: The Art Quilt* at the Grove Street Gallery in Worcester; it then tours.

1985

Workshop tour in England, Ireland, France, and Switzerland.
First trip to Italy; visits Venice and Verona.
Travel to Alaska; visits Denali National Park.
Begins *Rhythm/Color* series with *Spanish Dance*, commissioned by the Newark (NJ) Museum through a grant from the Louis Comfort Tiffany Foundation.

1986

Exhibits *Rhythm/Color: Morris Men* and *Rhythm/Color: Improvisation 3* in the exhibition *The Art Quilt* at the Los Angeles Municipal Art Gallery. Exhibition tours the U.S. Participates in the inaugural exhibition of the new American Craft Museum, *Craft Today: Poetry of the Physical*, with *Rhythm/Color: The Concord Cotillion*.

1987

Solo exhibition, *Michael James: New Quilts* takes place at the Wheeler Gallery in Providence, RI. Exhibits *Bias Cut*, *A View into Time/Motion*, *Leitmotif*, among others.

1988

Receives a Visual Artists' Fellowship as well as a USA/France Exchange Fellowship from the National Endowment for the Arts.
First European exhibition *Michael James: Nouveaux Quilts* takes place at the Galerie Jonas in Petit-Cortaillod, Near Neuchâtel, Switzerland. Workshops follow in France, Germany, Holland, and Switzerland.
Spends several days hiking along the Aletsch glacier in south-central Switzerland.

1989

Craft Today USA, organized by the American Craft Museum, begins 3-year European tour at the Musée des Arts Décoratifs du Louvre in Paris. Exhibits *Waves 2*. Begins construction of new studio.

1990

First trip to Japan, at the invitation of Nihon Vogue Company, Ltd.
Lectures and workshops in Tokyo and in Osaka. Visits Kyoto.
Completes *Sky/Wind Variations*, a four-part screen commissioned by the Massachusetts Mutual Life Insurance Company in Springfield, MA.
Solo show at Clark University Gallery, Worcester, MA subsequently travels to Galerie Jonas for second European solo exhibition.
Spends three months in artists' residency at the La Napoule Art Foundation at La Napoule, near Cannes, France, with five European and ten American artists. Works on paper exclusively, completing a series of oil pastel drawings.

1991

Begins working in new studio in July.
Aletsch is acquired by the museum of the American Quilter's Society.

1992

Awarded an honorary Doctor of Fine Arts Degree by his alma mater, the University of Massachusetts at Dartmouth (formerly Southeastern Massachusetts University).

1993

Inducted into the Quilter's Hall of Fame, Marion, Indiana.
The Quiltmaker's Handbook and *The Second Quiltmaker's Handbook*, both out-of-print since 1986, are re-published by Leone Publications.
First trips to Florence, Italy and Barcelona, Spain during workshop tour in France and Switzerland.
Waves 2 is acquired by the American Craft Museum, New York, NY.

1994

Among four recipients of the first biannual *Society of Arts and Crafts Award* sponsored by the Society of Arts and Crafts of Boston.
Quilt No. 150: Rehoboth Meander is acquired by the Renwick Gallery of the National Museum of American Art of the Smithsonian Institution, Washington, D.C.

1995

Third European solo exhibition takes place in June at Galerie Jonas, Petit-Cortaillod, Switzerland and coincides with the publication of *Michael James: Studio Quilts* by Editions Victor Attinger, SA of Neuchâtel.
The Metaphysics of Action: Entropic Forms receives a juror's citation in the 8th International Triennial of Tapestry at the Central Museum of Textiles in Lodz, Poland.
Travels to Scandinavia for workshops in Sweden, Norway, and Denmark. While in Oslo visits National Gallery of Art and encounters the museum's collection of 16th and 17th century Russian icons.

1996

In June, completes *Ikon*, the first of a new group of quilts marking a break from his "signature" style of the preceding dozen years.
Travels in Switzerland, the Netherlands, Germany, Denmark, and France center around workshop engagements. Returns to Florence, Italy and visits San Gimignano and Arezzo.

1997

Rhythm/Color: Bacchanal and *Crash Site* acquired by the American Craft Museum, New York, NY.
Rhythm/Color: Improvisation 2 acquired by the Mint Museum of Art, Charlotte, North Carolina.
Participates on the jury of the first "European Art Quilts" exhibition at the Nederlands Textile Museum in Tilburg, the Netherlands.
Conducts workshops and lectures in Great Britain; in London he and his wife Judy celebrate their twenty-fifth wedding anniversary.
Michael James: Studio Quilts nominated for the Patricia and Philip Frost Prize for distinguished scholarship in American Crafts, sponsored by the Renwick Gallery of the National Museum of American Art, Washington, D.C.

awards

1978

National Endowment for the Arts Fellowship

1979

Boston Artists Foundation Fellowship, Massachusetts

1985

"Fund for the Arts" Grant award for joint exhibition at the Society of Arts and Crafts, Boston, Massachusetts

1988

National Endowment for the Arts Fellowship
Boston Artists' Foundation Fellowship, Massachusetts

1990

USA/France Exchange Fellowship, National Endowment for the Arts and the La Napoule Art Foundation, La Napoule, France; 3-month residency, September to December.

1992

Honorary Doctorate, University of Massachusetts at Dartmouth

1993

Inducted into the Quilter's Hall of Fame, Marion, Indiana

1994

The Society of Arts and Crafts Award, Boston, Massachusetts

1997

Finalist grant from the New England Foundation for the Arts.

one-man exhibitions

1977

Visual Arts Gallery, Bridgewater State College, Bridgewater, Massachusetts

1978

Visual Arts Gallery, Ohio University, Lancaster, Ohio

1980

LeMoyne Art Foundation, Inc., Tallahassee, Florida

1983

The Worcester Craft Center, Worcester, Massachusetts

1984

Space Galllery, Western Michigan University, Kalamazoo, Michigan

1987

The Wheeler Gallery, Providence, Rhode Island

1988

Galerie Jonas, Petit-Cortaillod, Switzerland

1990

Galerie Jonas, Petit-Cortaillod, Switzerland
Clark University Gallery, Worcester, Massachsetts

1993

Marion Public Library, Marion, Indiana

1995

Galerie Jonas, Petit-Cortaillod, Switzerland

selected group exhibitions

1975

DeCordova Museum, Lincoln, Massachusetts, *Bed and Board*
Boston Center for the Arts, Boston, Massachusetts, *Quilts for '76*

1976

Brockton Art Center, Brockton, Massachusetts, *Craftforms*
Boston City Hall Gallery, Boston, Massachusetts, *Three Centuries of Massachusetts Quilts*

1977

Museum of Contemporary Crafts, New York, New York, *Young Americans: Wood, Plastic, Fiber, Leather*
International Exhibitions Foundation, Washington, D.C., *American Quiltmakers*
Society of Arts and Crafts, Boston, Massachusetts, *Show of Hands*
Danforth Library Gallery, New England College, Henniker, New Hampshire, *Third Edition, Ltd.*

1978

Bruce Gallery. Edinboro State College, Edinboro, Pennsylvania, *Intent '78: Fabrics*
Danforth Library Gallery, New England College, Henniker, New Hampshire, *Fourth Edition: New Horizons.*
Brockton Art Center, Brockton, Massachusetts, *The Object: Form Follows Function*
Brockton Art Center, Brockton, Massachusetts, *Hearts and Flowers*
Hunter Museum of Art, Chattanooga, Tennessee, *The Little Quilt*

1979

Worcester Craft Center, Worcester, Massachusetts, *Craftsmen's Fellowship Exhibition*
Stedelijk Museum, Schiedam, Holland, *American Quiltmakers*

1980

American Craft Museum, New York, New York, *Art for Use*

1981

The Dairy Barn Cultural Arts Center, Athens, Ohio, *Quilt National '81*
Kenyon College, Gambier, Ohio, *Contemporary Quilts*
Southern Alleghenies Museum of Art, Loretto, Pennsylvania, *The New Quilt*

1982

American Crafts Museum, New York, New York, *Pattern*

1983

Dairy Barn Cultural Arts Center, Athens, Ohio, *Quilt National '83*

1984

Musée Chateau d' Annecy, France and tour *Quilts Contemporains Américains*

Asahi Shimbun and APT, Inc., Tokyo, Japan and tour *Contemporary American Quilts*

1986

American Crafts Museum, New York, New York and tour *Craft Today: Poetry of the Physical*

Los Angeles Municipal Art Gallery, California and tour *The Art Quilt*

Society of Arts and Crafts, Boston, Massachusetts, *Constructions* (Fund for the Arts Award exhibition)

University Student Center Gallery, North Carolina State University, Raleigh, North Carolina, *Color: The Spectrum of Expression*

1987

The Dairy Barn Cultural Arts Center, Athens, Ohio, *Quilt National '87*

1989

Musée des Arts Décoratifs du Louvre, Paris, France and tour *Craft Today USA*

1991

Artists Foundation Gallery, Boston, Massachusetts, *Vessels and Textiles: Ancient Forms, New Visions*

The Dairy Barn Cultural Arts Center, Athens, Ohio, *Quilt National '91*

Northern Virginia Fine Arts Association at The Athenaeum, Alexandria, Virginia, *Contemporary Quilts*

Chelsea Gallery, Hinds University Center, Western Carolina University, Cullowhee, North Carolina, *Contemporary Quilts: Seven Innovative Artists*

1992

San Diego Historical Society Museum, California, *Visions: The Art of the Quilt*

The Works Gallery, Philadelphia, Pennsylvania, *Color, Light, and Motion*

1993

University Art Gallery, University of Massachusetts at Dartmouth, *Another View: Work by Visiting Artists in Clay, Metal, Wood, Fiber*

Crafts Council, London, England and tour *Contemporary American Quilts*

1994

Society of Arts and Crafts, Boston, Massachusetts, four-person "Society of Arts and Crafts Award" show

Kurts Bingham Gallery, Memphis, Tennessee, *Studio Quilts: A Memphis Invitational Exhibition of Contemporary Quilts*

1995

8th International Triennial of Tapestry, Central Museum of Textiles, Lodz, Poland

1996

Worcester Center for Crafts, Worcester, MA, *New Traditions '96*

Wheeler Gallery, Providence, RI, *Recent Work*, two-person exhibition with jeweler Klaus Bürgel

1997

Gross McCleaf Gallery, Philadelphia, PA, *Contemporary Quilts*

Kunstindustrie Museum, Copenhagen, Denmark, *Celebrating American Craft*

Everson Museum, Syracuse, NY, *Innovation: Growth and Diversity*

American Craft museum, New York, NY, *On the Cutting Edge: Quilts from the Collection*

other fine books from C&T Publishing

An Amish Adventure: 2nd Edition, Roberta Horton

Anatomy of a Doll: The Fabric Sculptor's Handbook, Susanna Oroyan

Appliqué 12 Easy Ways! Elly Sienkiewicz

The Art of Silk Ribbon Embroidery, Judith Baker Montano

The Artful Ribbon, Candace Kling

Baltimore Beauties and Beyond (Volume I), Elly Sienkiewicz

Basic Seminole Patchwork, Cheryl Greider Bradkin

Beyond the Horizon: Small Landscape Appliqué, Valerie Hearder

Buttonhole Stitch Appliqué, Jean Wells

A Colorful Book, Yvonne Porcella

Colors Changing Hue, Yvonne Porcella

Crazy Quilt Handbook, Judith Montano

Crazy Quilt Odyssey, Judith Montano

Crazy with Cotton, Diana Leone

Deidre Scherer: Work in Fabric & Thread, Deidre Scherer

Dimensional Appliqué: Baskets, Blooms & Baltimore Borders,
    Elly Sienkiewicz

Elegant Stitches: An Illustrated Stitch Guide & Source Book of
    Inspiration, Judith Baker Montano

Enduring Grace: Quilts from the Shelburne Museum Collection,
    Celia Y. Oliver

Everything Flowers: Quilts from the Garden, Jean and Valori Wells

The Fabric Makes the Quilt, Roberta Horton

Faces & Places: Images in Appliqué, Charlotte Warr Andersen

Fantastic Figures: Ideas & Techniques Using the New Clays,
    Susanna Oroyan

Forever Yours, Wedding Quilts, Clothing & Keepsakes,
    Amy Barickman

Fractured Landscape Quilts, Katie Pasquini Masopust

From Fiber to Fabric: The Essential Guide to Quiltmaking Textiles,
    Harriet Hargrave

Hand Quilting with Alex Anderson: Six Projects for Hand Quilters,
    Alex Anderson

Heirloom Machine Quilting, Third Edition, Harriet Hargrave

Imagery on Fabric, Second Edition, Jean Ray Laury

Impressionist Palette, Gai Perry

Impressionist Quilts, Gai Perry

Judith B. Montano: Art & Inspirations, Judith B. Montano

Kaleidoscopes & Quilts, Paula Nadelstern

Mariner's Compass Quilts, New Directions, Judy Mathieson

Mastering Machine Appliqué, Harriet Hargrave

The New Sampler Quilt, Diana Leone

On the Surface: Thread Embellishment & Fabric Manipulation,
    Wendy Hill

Papercuts and Plenty, Vol. III of Baltimore Beauties and Beyond,
    Elly Sienkiewicz

Patchwork Persuasion: Fascinating Quilts from Traditional Designs,
    Joen Wolfrom

Patchwork Quilts Made Easy, Jean Wells (co-published with
    Rodale Press, Inc.)

Pattern Play, Doreen Speckmann

Pieced Clothing Variations, Yvonne Porcella

Pieces of an American Quilt, Patty McCormick

Piecing: Expanding the Basics, Ruth B. McDowell

Plaids & Stripes: The Use of Directional Fabrics in Quilts,
    Roberta Horton

Quilts for Fabric Lovers, Alex Anderson

Quilts from the Civil War: Nine Projects, Historical Notes, Diary
    Entries, Barbara Brackman

Quilts, Quilts, and More Quilts! Diana McClun and Laura Nownes

Recollections, Judith Baker Montano

Ruth B. McDowell: Art & Inspirations, Ruth B. McDowell

Say It with Quilts, Diana McClun and Laura Nownes

Simply Stars: Quilts that Sparkle, Alex Anderson

Six Color World: Color, Cloth, Quilts & Wearables, Yvonne Porcella

Small Scale Quiltmaking: Precision, Proportion, and Detail,
    Sally Collins

Soft-Edge Piecing, Jinny Beyer

Start Quilting with Alex Anderson: Six Projects for First-Time Quilters,
    Alex Anderson

Stripes in Quilts, Mary Mashuta

Tradition with a Twist: Variations on Your Favorite Quilts,
    Blanche Young and Dalene Young Stone

Trapunto by Machine, Hari Walner

The Visual Dance: Creating Spectacular Quilts, Joen Wolfrom

Wildflowers: Designs for Appliqué & Quilting, Carol Armstrong

Willowood: Further Adventures in Buttonhole Stitch Appliqué,
    Jean Wells

For more information write for a free catalog:
C&T Publishing, Inc.
P.O. Box 1456, Lafayette, CA 94549
(800) 284-1114
http://www.ctpub.com
e-mail: ctinfo@ctpub.com

For quilting supplies:
Cotton Patch Mail Order
3405 Hall Lane, Dept. CTB, Lafayette, CA 94549
e-mail: cottonpa@aol.com
(800) 835-4418
(510) 283-7883

ART & INSPIRATIONS

author

Michael James is internationally recognized as one of the leading innovators in quiltmaking today. For the last twenty years, he has devoted himself to exploring the creative possibilities inherent in the pieced quilt. In a medium still heavily rooted in the past, he has worked with a visionary's dedication to showing what quilts can be.

contributors

Patricia Harris and **David Lyon** have collaborated as journalists and critics since 1980. As frequent contributors to *Fiberarts*, they have reviewed numerous quilt exhibitions and have profiled artists who work in fiber media. They have also written for *American Craft*, *Crafts Report*, and regional and national general-interest magazines. Since the early 1980s, Harris and Lyon have been covering the evolution of contemporary quilt-art with a special interest in the work of Michael James.

Harris received her bachelor's degree from Harvard University and did post-graduate study in art history at the Minneapolis Institute of Art. She spent nine years as an administrator with the Massachusetts Council on the Arts and Humanities, where she coordinated funding programs for the visual arts and crafts disciplines. Lyon received a bachelor's degree from the University of Maine and a master of fine arts from the University of Massachusetts. He spent a decade managing a literary publishing house.

Patricia Malarcher is the editor of *The Surface Design Journal*. Her articles have also been published in *American Craft*, *Fiberarts*, *The New York Times*, and other publications.

A recipient of a James Renwick Fellowship for research in contemporary craft, she also is an artist whose works have been shown internationally.

index

ART & INSPIRATIONS